Brian McNaught's Guide on LGBTQ Issues In the Workplace

"What if I have employees with religious differences?"
"What if I don't know the correct language to use?"
"What if it's an unwelcoming environment?"

Brian McNaught's Guide on LGBTQ Issues In the Workplace

INTRODUCTION

The guidance offered in this book represents four decades of working with audiences on lesbian, gay, bisexual, transgender, and queer issues in a multitude of settings around the world. Each word of this guide has been vetted by a large group of professionals in the field, representing life experiences as teachers, diversity directors, trainers, and LGBTQ advocates. That doesn't mean that the reader won't get a different point of view or advice from someone who is lesbian, gay, bisexual, transgender, or queer. The trick in successfully navigating the waters is being open to learning new things, and knowing that just as you think you've got it, you'll hear a new perspective.

A great deal has changed in Western culture since this guide was created as a Web resource for corporate managers. The most significant change is in the increased comfort level most people have with homosexuality and bisexuality. More heterosexual people know, love, respect and affirm gay, lesbian, and bisexual people than was true even a few years ago. And the experience of being transgender is more widely understood by cis-gender (not transgender) people because of personal contact, and increased visibility in the media. One trend, however, that has taken hold, and is much less understood by the general public, especially people my age, is the self-labeling as queer, and the emergence of non-binary thinking about orientation and gender.

Many young people tell us they are queer, meaning a number of things. Some people, young and old, including those in academia and in the LGBTQ media, use the word "queer" to represent being lesbian, gay, bisexual, transgender, and other experiences of sexual attraction and gender identity and expression.

Other people use the word "queer" to communicate that they live in a non-binary world, not divided by orientation or gender. They don't see identifying as male or female as accurate to their experience. They might refer to themselves as gender queer. Others feel the same about sexual or affectional attraction. They are not gay, lesbian, bisexual, or straight. They are "other" on a continuum. The word "queer" fits best for them.

What does this mean to managing the workplace? It depends upon the setting. I recently attended a lesbian, gay, bisexual, transgender, and queer (LGBTQ) religious conference at which participants were asked to first state their name, and then which pronouns they prefer to be called. It's no longer "she and her," or "he and him." The most common substitutes are "them and their." At Harvard University, students can request that professors refer to them as "ze" among other options.

How is this a workplace issue? Because, organizations tell their employees to "bring your whole selves to work." In most places, team building requires that each person feel safe and valued. Depending upon the individual importance of the word "queer" to self-identification, it's not unlikely that pronouns will have to be discussed sooner rather than later. Some people ask that "him or her" always be replaced by "their." You will notice the effort to be sensitive to those feelings in this document.

The speed with which this new cultural phenomena makes its way into the organization, its day to day business, and its approach to recruiting, hiring, and diversity guidelines will depend in large part on how many people put a face on the name "queer," and how important to the success of the organization the self-identifying queer person is. If a person who refers to themselves as queer is also the employee who brings in the most money, policies, attitudes, and behaviors will change quickly.

The best strategy for managing this workplace issue is to be patient, open, flexible, interested, and informed, as you were, or must be, in responding to lesbian, gay, bisexual, and transgender issues, and all others, such as race, gender, disability, and faith that are interconnected.

TABLE OF CONTENTS

Introduction

Overview:

* The Organization's Goals

* The Law

* What the Terms Mean

* What Gay, Lesbian, Bisexual, Transgender, and Queer Employees Need

* What is Expected of Every Employee

* What is Expected of Every Manager

* "So What If…?" (Answers for Managers)

…I don't know how to communicate the organization's position?
…I disagree with the organization's policy on this?
…I don't know the proper language?
…I don't know what constitutes discrimination or harassment?
…I don't know how to behave proactively?
…I have employees with conservative religious values?
…someone quotes the Bible or the Koran to me?
…I'm dealing with cultural conflicts?
…the law in my country prohibits homosexual behavior?
…my boss is hostile to the issue?
…our best client is homophobic or transphobic?
…our best client won't work with our lesbian, gay, bisexual, transgender, or queer employee?
…someone in my group comes out to me?
…someone I think is gay won't come out?
…someone in the group is transgender?
…my organization doesn't have a policy on gender identity or expression?
…a lesbian, gay, bisexual, transgender or queer employee wants to be out and I think it's unsafe?
…a lesbian, gay, bisexual, transgender, or queer employee tells a LGBTQ joke or uses prohibited language?

...I don't have any lesbian, gay, bisexual, transgender, or queer people in my group or client base?
...the lesbian, gay, bisexual, transgender, or queer person's job performance is the problem?
...the transgender or queer person wants to use the "wrong" bathroom?
...we need training and someone refuses to participate?
...legal action is threatened?
...I'm lesbian, gay, bisexual, or queer?
...I'm transgender or queer?
...the organization isn't a safe place for LGBTQ people?
...the office of Human Resources is of no help to me?
...I manage lesbian, gay, bisexual, transgender, or queer people in a country with hostile cultural attitudes on the issues?
...I want to transfer a lesbian, gay, bisexual, transgender, or queer employee to an office in a country with hostile cultural attitudes on the issues?
...the lesbian, gay, bisexual, transgender, or queer person I want to transfer has a spouse/partner?
...I have a parent, or a spouse, of a LGBTQ person, and they need
   support?
...I want to recruit talented gay, lesbian, bisexual, transgender, or queer
   employees?
...I want to be an ally?
...I need outside help?

*Bottom Line

*About the Author

OVERVIEW

In their attempt to attract and retain the best and brightest employees in a global economy and multi-cultural workforce, organizations worldwide today speak in terms of *valuing* diversity, not tolerating it; of *empowering* the uniqueness each person brings to the table, not accommodating their differences.

To achieve their goals, organizations have written non-discrimination policies that exceed the legal guidelines of most nations. They have expanded their definition of "family" so that all of their employees receive equal benefits. They have fostered the creation of resource or business groups for their minority, or under-represented employees, and they are providing diversity training to all employees.

Of all of these efforts, classes that provide the understanding, and the tools, that are the most effective in helping to create a workplace that feels safe and productive for everyone. There is no substitute for a good, comprehensive education in bridging the gap between organizational policy and organizational culture. However, to be successful, these classes **must** have the complete support of the organization's leadership not only in words, but also in deeds. The programs **must** have executive sponsorship, and managers **must** know that they are being held accountable for their efforts to promote the organization's diversity initiatives.

Therefore, people at all levels of responsibility need to know: the organization's goals, the reason for the policies, the law, what the terms mean, what the employees are looking for from their employer, what is expected by the organization of every employee and every manager, and guidelines on what behaviors create, and what behaviors destroy workplace cohesion.

This reference guide has been written not as a substitute for, but rather as a complement to training. It is written to help you respond confidently and competently to concerns related to gay, lesbian, bisexual, transgender, and queer workplace issues as they arise.

Background on Lesbian, Gay, Bisexual, Transgender, and Queer Issues

If you have attended diversity training on these topics, this will serve as a review. If not, it provides a basic foundation that you will need to digest before being able to respond to any specific problems.

* Organizational goals – what are they, and why are they?
* The law
* What the terms mean
* What gay, lesbian, bisexual, transgender, and queer employees want
* What is expected of every employee
* What is expected of every manager

Organizational Goals:

There are a rapidly-increasing number of places in the world where discrimination based upon sexual orientation, and upon gender identity and expression, are strictly prohibited. But your organization has compelling business reasons for prohibiting discrimination that go well beyond legal compliance. It does so to achieve its organizational goals, which are set to reflect the realities of a global labor pool and marketplace that demand respect and inclusion of all members.

Laws at the national and local level may or may not prohibit discrimination based upon sexual orientation and gender identity and expression. These ever-changing laws vary from country to country, and if we listed the existing legislation, our list would be out of date before this book is completed. If the laws on these issues concern you, consult your Legal department or use the Internet to find out "laws on sexual orientation and gender identity and expression in…" Oklahoma City, London, Singapore, Dubai, etc.

The motivating factor in most major organizations in having such non-discrimination and anti-harassment policies is that if they don't, they lose the search for talent and the ability to remain competitive. What talented lesbian, gay, bisexual, transgender, or queer person would willingly work where he, she, or they isn't/aren't wanted or protected? That's true for all other under-represented groups as well. In an unwelcoming work environment, productivity and profitability are significantly sacrificed, as is a potential client base.

Think of competition as a **tug of war**. Your organization and its major competitor both get to pick your ten best employees to represent you. These ten people happen to reflect your diverse workforce, so the hands on your end of the rope may be black, brown, red, yellow, and white, male, female, and other, belonging to a fundamentalist Christian, Muslim, Jew, agnostic, or atheist, who are gay, straight, bisexual, transgender, or queer, and with disabilities that are seen or unseen, who speak every language imaginable, and who have other differences we haven't even begun to think about.

To get them to pull as a team and to win the competition, each one has to trust that he, she, or other is safe, physically and emotionally, and valued; that at the end of the day, they are going to be evaluated on the basis of their skills and performance and on no other factors; and that the organization really does celebrate their unique contribution.

If any of the ten people let go of the rope or decide not to give pulling it their best effort, the competition, which incidentally is now reading the same guide you are, WINS. If that happens, morale goes down, as does the value of the organization's stock, and your value as a manager to the organization.

A manager's job is to ensure that their team members not only have the incentive and skills they need to perform their jobs, but also the environment they need to work happily – or as happily as can be expected when they're not on vacation.

That's why the organization emphasizes "inclusion" and its desire to *value* diversity. They don't just want to attract the best talent; they want to *retain* the best talent. In doing so, the organization raises its competitive position by increasing its productivity, thereby ensuring higher profitability.

My partner in life was one of the best and brightest at his Wall Street firm where he was a managing director, but took an early retirement because he felt *tolerated* at work, not *supported*. It was the small things that got to him, like watching everyone else get asked about their weekend plans, but not him. People weren't hostile, but their discomfort with homosexuality came through in their avoidance of discussing anything personal with him.

Not only did they lose a loyal, hardworking, revenue-producing, effective manager, but they also lost someone who could have guided them in their dealings with LGBTQ staff and clients, and with the countless number of heterosexuals for whom LGBTQ people and issues are important. They subsequently had to retrain an employee to take his place, and to wait until another gay employee dared to come out and become available to tap as a resource in securing their share of the gay dollar.

What a difference "Good morning, Ray. How was your weekend?" would have made.

The Law:

We've talked briefly about the laws that prohibit discrimination based upon sexual orientation and gender identity and expression, but what about the laws that prohibit homosexuality and/or transgenderism? How does an organization comply with such laws but also stay true to its own mission and policies?

Think of homosexuality, heterosexuality, and bisexuality as having three components. The first is **orientation**. That's what we *feel* sexually. The second is **behavior**. That's what we **do** sexually. The third is **identity**. That's what we **call ourselves** sexually.

Laws that prohibit homosexuality only concern sexual **behavior**. Organizations take no positions on anyone's private behavior. The status of being homosexual and of saying that one is lesbian, gay, bisexual, or queer is what is protected and valued by organizational policy, just as the status of being and identifying oneself as Muslim, Jew, and fundamentalist Christian is what is protected and valued. Your organization doesn't concern itself with whether or not the Muslim prays daily, the Jew goes to temple, or the fundamentalist Christian reads the Bible at home.

The trend today is that more and more countries are prohibiting workplace discrimination that is based on sexual orientation and on gender expression and identity, and the handful of countries that have laws against same-sex behavior and against transitioning, or realigning, one's body to match one's gender, generally do not interfere with the business practices of multinational organizations.

What the Terms Mean:

Using proper terminology communicates that you are competent and confident on the issues facing gay, lesbian, bisexual, transgender, and queer employees. Some words, when heard by LGBTQ people, create immediate trust. Other words, when used by a heterosexual or cis-gender person can be like fingernails on a chalkboard. They are irritating and they diminish trust. And then there are words which when used are not experienced by the lesbian, gay, bisexual, transgender, or queer person as hostile, but rather as unfortunate.

A few years ago, the Director of Human Resources at a major international organization greeted me with the proud assurance, "We do a good job here dealing with alternative lifestyles." I replied with a smile, as I know he meant no offense, "Can this be a teachable moment?" When he said "Yes, of course," I explained that my being gay was neither an alternative nor a lifestyle. It's a life, unchosen but nevertheless embraced as good, healthy, and normal.

Choosing no word or the wrong word to make a point can create the impression of bias. For instance, some people with a gay sibling will say, "My brother is one." One *what*? A magician? By not using the word "gay," the straight sibling unintentionally communicates embarrassment. Other heterosexual relatives sometimes say, "My cousin admitted that she was lesbian." Does one *admit* that they won the lottery? Or, instead do they *admit* they broke the lamp? We admit to things that are bad, so the choice of the word *admit* suggests bias.

As we all grow in our understanding of what words are useful in creating a welcoming environment, and what words are not useful in doing the same, it's important to have a sense of humor, patience with ourselves and others, and expectations of progress, not perfection. It is better to make a mistake trying to use the right words in reaching out to a gay, lesbian, bisexual, transgender, or queer colleague than it is to clam up out of fear of being politically incorrect and unintentionally communicating discomfort with your colleagues.

So, what are the useful words, and what are the words that aren't so helpful in creating a safe and productive work environment? I offer here the words with which I am comfortable and knowledgeable. For further counsel, seek guidance from the lesbian, gay, bisexual, transgender, and queer people in your organization or area.

Let's start with the words *homophobia, transphobia* and *heterosexism.*

Homophobia is commonly understood as the fear and hatred of homosexuality in ourselves or in others. Regrettably, some of the most outspoken anti-gay voices are covering up feelings of shame. At its worst, homophobia is manifested as physical violence and emotional abuse. Once, when I came downstairs from my apartment on my way to work, there was a large, handmade sign taped to the wall over all of the mailboxes that read, "Get out of town McNaught. I hope you die of AIDS." That's homophobia. The intention is to make you uncomfortable coming out as lesbian, gay, bisexual, transgender, or queer, or as an ally of LGBTQ people. Homophobic people go out of their way to create an unwelcoming or hostile environment. Simply having conservative religious views or being uncomfortable with the subject of homosexuality doesn't make a person homophobic.

Transphobia is understood as the fear and hatred of people whose gender identity or gender expression is inconsistent with what the observing person expects, or with which they are comfortable. Transphobic responses, like homophobic responses, fall on a continuum, from physical violence (often against men who cross-dress), to social pressure to conform to cultural expectations of "appropriate" masculine and feminine behaviors. Additionally, most people think in the binary concept of male or female. Choose one and stick with it. But queer people experience themselves on the continuum between male and female. They are both and neither. Further, they don't respond well to "him" or "her." It's best to ask, "With which pronouns are you most comfortable?"

Heterosexism is a value system based upon the assumption that nature or God intended for there only to be heterosexuals, and that homosexuals and bisexuals are thus a mistake to be tolerated but not validated or valued. It's also a belief that everyone is heterosexual unless a person tells you that they're lesbian, gay, bisexual, or queer, or fit cultural stereotypes. Making such assumptions is dangerous. In one organization in which I worked as a trainer, 76% of the lesbian, gay, and bisexual employees reported having been told an anti-gay joke by someone who thought that they were heterosexual. And it's not just lesbian, gay, bisexual, and queer people who are invisible. So too are their parents, siblings, children, and friends, all of whom are offended by anti-gay comments. The same holds true of the family and friends of transgender people. They're offended by anti-transgender jokes or slurs.

To create an environment in which people don't feel the need to be invisible, I suggest using the words: **Gay, lesbian, bisexual, transgender, queer, transsexual, cross dresser, homosexual, sexual orientation, gender identity, gender expression, spouse, partner,** and **life partner.**

Don't use the words: "sexual preference," or "alternative lifestyle" to refer to lesbian, gay, bisexual, or queer people, or to their sexual orientation, and **don't** refer to the spouse or partner of a gay man or lesbian woman as their "friend" or "roommate." **Don't** speak of coming out as the person "admitting" being gay. Nor should the word "choice" be used to describe why a person is lesbian, gay bisexual, transgender, or queer.

Men who are **gay** are gay men. The word "gay" here is best used as an adjective. **Gay** is not a sexual term. It describes a person, not a behavior.

Women who are gay are **lesbian**, or gay women. **Lesbian** is not a sexual term. It describes a person, not a behavior.

People who are **bisexual** are bisexual men or bisexual women. The word "bisexual" doesn't suggest that the person has sex with both genders, but rather they have the capacity to be attracted to both genders, in varying degrees.

Homosexual is not an inappropriate word but most people who are homosexual prefer the term **lesbian, gay,** or **queer**. To them, "homosexual" feels formal, academic, and medical, (just as the term "transvestite" does for people who cross-dress.) For me, the word *homosexual* feels like "Mr. McNaught." The word *gay* feels like "Brian."

We all have a **sexual orientation**, *not* a sexual preference. No one *chooses* their sexual feelings, thus *preference* is not involved. The term "sexual preference" makes it sound as if the discrimination that is experienced could be eliminated if only the lesbian, gay, bisexual, or queer person would *prefer* to be heterosexual.

Don't say "alternative lifestyle," or "lifestyle" in reference to being lesbian, gay, bisexual, transgender, or queer. None are lifestyles. They're *lives*. The word "lifestyle" suggests something chosen and changeable. There is no such thing as a heterosexual or Christian lifestyle.

Lesbian, gay, bisexual, and queer people are able to legally marry or enter civil unions with their same-sex partner in many countries, so the term often used to refer to their mate is **spouse**. The terms **"partner"** and **"life partner"** are also used. If in doubt about a person's sexual orientation and relational status, use *inclusive* language, and ask them if they have a *partner* or a *significant other*. Once you learn that they are gay or lesbian, you can ask if they have a **boyfriend** or **girlfriend**. Never call a lesbian, gay, or queer person's partner their *roommate* or *friend*. Doing so diminishes the significance of their relationship as it would for a person in a heterosexual relationship.

Don't assume that the word "queer" is the preferred term of an employee. The term can be offensive to gay men and women, particularly those who grew up with it being used as a derogatory word against them.

Don't use the words or expressions: "MTF" (male to female) "FTM" (female to male) or "Tranny," to refer to transgender people, even if you hear lesbian, gay, bisexual, transgender or queer people doing so. Don't use the word "transvestite" to describe a person who cross-dresses. Say instead "a person who cross-dresses." Regarding pronouns, the transgender person appreciates being referred to as "she" or "her" when their gender identity or expression is female, and "he" or "him" when their gender identity or expression is male. If you don't know what pronouns a person prefers, ask.

Don't ask a transgender person whether or not they have had sex realignment surgery. Some transgender people may offer that information, but it's a very private matter. A transgender person should be considered a woman or a man based upon her or his presentation of themselves, not on their surgical status.

Transgender takes in both *gender identity* (an inner sense of being male, female, or other,) and *gender expression* (how we manifest feeling masculine, feminine, or androgynous through the way we look, act, or dress). The word transgender (NOT *transgendered*) is best used as an adjective that is employed as an umbrella term. Included under the *transgender* umbrella are **transsexuals** (an adjective and a noun) who most often transition or realign to live full-time in the gender other than the one assigned at birth, **intersex** people who were/are born with medical conditions that make their anatomical sex unclear, **bi-gendered, gender-queer**, or **androgynous** people who see themselves on a gender identity continuum, and **cross-dressing** people who wear the clothing of the other gender some of the time. It is popularly believed, though difficult to prove, that most cross dressers are heterosexual males, just as most left-handed people are heterosexual. Gender identity/expression and sexual attraction are two *very* different things. One shouldn't make assumptions about the sexual orientation of a transgender person.

Try not to overuse the acronym LGBTQ or GLBTQ, even if you hear lesbian, gay, bisexual, transgender, and queer people use it frequently. It stands for lesbian, gay, bisexual, transgender, and queer, but always using the letters is not helpful in breaking down the fear some people have of the words "gay," "lesbian," "bisexual," "transgender," and "queer," nor is it respectful of the diversity among the groups which are represented by the acronym. We don't say BLA for blacks, Latinos, and Asians.

If you have doubts about what term to use, ask a member of your local lesbian, gay, bisexual, transgender and queer Employee Resource Group (ERG) or your Human Resources professional or Diversity specialist. You can also search the Internet for "National Gay (or Transgender) Organizations in…" and insert your country. E-mail the organization and ask for guidance on terminology. You can also write to me at brian@brian-mcnaught.com.

Becoming culturally competent requires some homework but it pays off. Here are some facts and symbols that are good to know. **Gay Pride Month** or **Gay Awareness Month** is in June in the United States, and many other countries, to commemorate the June 28 revolt that took place at the **Stonewall Inn** on Christopher Street in Greenwich Village. The police were conducting a routine raid in which bar patrons were led into police wagons and transported to jail. The patrons this time revolted, refusing to be manhandled, and began throwing bottles at the police, who took refuge in the bar. Many historians cite the revolt at Stonewall as the beginning of the modern day Gay Rights Movement. The Stonewall Inn is now a National Monument.

October 11 is **National Coming Out Day** in the United States. It began in 1988 as the anniversary of the 1987 March on Washington.

October is **LGBTQ History Month** in the United States. It was first celebrated in 1994, founded by a Missouri high school history teacher, Rodney Wilson. The month was chosen to coincide with National Coming Out Day.

Transgender Day of Remembrance is observed annually on November 20 to memorialize those whose lives were lost in acts of anti-transgender violence.

Rainbow Flag

There are other rainbow flags, used by other groups and cultures, to celebrate peace, diversity, and even the Andean people. But the gay pride rainbow flag has become widely known and recognized as the international symbol of the gay, lesbian, bisexual, transgender, and queer community. The gay pride rainbow flag, which contains six colored stripes, with red at the top, is sometimes called the freedom flag.

Transgender Pride Flag

Known and used less often, the transgender pride flag was created in 1999 to symbolize pride and the struggle for transgender rights. The flag employs stripes of baby blue and baby pink to represent male and female, and white to symbolize intersex.

Pink Triangle

The Nazis used the pink triangle, sown on clothing inside and outside of concentration camps, to designate and shame the person as a male homosexual. With the point facing down, the pink triangle was adopted after the war as a symbol of remembrance and solidarity. Next to the rainbow flag, it is the second most popular symbol of the gay, lesbian, bisexual, transgender, and queer communities.

Transgender Symbol

There is more than one transgender symbol, all of which combine variations of the medical signs for male and female. The most popular symbol shows the traditional male symbol of the circle with the arrow at the top right, the female symbol of the cross at the bottom of the circle, and a combination of both symbols, an arrow with a cross bar, at the top left.

What Gay, Lesbian, Bisexual, Transgender, Queer Employees Need:

That's easy. They need the same thing every other employee needs – to feel safe and valued, to get equal pay for equal work, and to be able to bring their full selves to work. They need to be able to put a picture of the person they love on their desk or as a screensaver on their computer if they so choose, to socialize with their colleagues, to have the unique perspective they bring to the workplace appreciated, and to be seen as an important component of the team. Gay, lesbian, bisexual, transgender, and queer people need the organization to acknowledge and affirm the diversity represented by their families. They need spousal benefits, to have their partner's relocation expenses covered, and to receive parental leave when adopting or having a child. Transgender and queer people need to be able to use a restroom that is convenient, safe, and dignified. No one is looking for *special* treatment, just equal treatment. Lesbian, gay, bisexual, transgender, and queer people who are able to be out at work are far more productive because they spend much less time and energy hiding who they are. They are also far more loyal to the organization than are LGBTQ people who feel that they can't come out at work, and if they dare do so, will no longer be safe and valued.

What is Expected of Every Employee:

Every employee is expected to *proactively* embrace the organization's values of inclusion. The organization is hiring more than an individual who has a valuable knowledge or skill. They are also hiring a *team member* who will treat every other team member with professional respect and courtesy. More than refraining from engaging in destructive behaviors, all employees are expected to *actively* participate in the creation of a cohesive workforce.

The only way the organization will succeed in its efforts to be optimally competitive is if every single employee sees as their personal responsibility the need to value diversity and to manifest behaviors and attitudes that achieve that goal.

That does not mean that every employee has to personally agree with company policy and practices, nor does the employee have to change any personal beliefs. But they must understand that they cannot impose their beliefs on their colleagues in any manner, nor give the impression that they are unsupportive of the organization's goals.

Think about the difference between values and behaviors as the difference in a song between the **words** and the **music**. Your organization has great *words* on valuing diversity, but what is its *music*? Do employees *feel* valued when they come to work? What "music" do they pick up from their manager, their colleagues, and from support staff?

The music is created by our behaviors, active and passive, toward other people. Avoidance does not create welcoming music. The organization expects its employees to mirror their positive words with positive personal music.

As an example, recall if you would the wonderful film by Steven Spielberg called *E.T.* In the beginning of the story, young Elliot knows that there is something alive in the garden shed. Rather than storm the building or yell at it "Come out of there!" he made a trail of Reese's Pieces candy from the shed to the house. Elliot took positive steps to create trust. That was his *music*. And it worked, didn't it? E.T. followed the candy to Elliot and they created a friendship. In their effort to *proactively* create an environment of trust, employees are urged to ask themselves, "What are *my* Reese's Pieces?" "What am I doing to make it easier for others to feel safe and valued at work?"

What is Expected of Every Manager:

Managers at every level are expected to represent the organization's values in all work-related situations, with employees and with clients. Their job performance is measured by their ability to create a cohesive team of diverse individuals that produces optimally because it respects individual differences. It is the manager's job to proactively create an environment in which each and every employee feels safe and valued. Any behaviors engaged in by the manager or by their employees that contribute to an unwelcoming work environment are contrary to the organization's goals and must be addressed immediately. Managers should always assume that there are lesbian, gay bisexual, transgender, and queer people present among their team members and among their clients. They should treat all disruptive behaviors equally, regardless of whether they are motivated by racism, sexism, homophobia, heterosexism, or transphobia. It is better to be overly cautious than casual about possible harassment. If the manager has doubts about what is expected of them with regard to creating a welcoming environment for lesbian, gay, bisexual, transgender, and queer employees and clients, and how to do so, they should seek guidance from their Diversity specialist or their Human Resources professional.

"So, What If…?" Recommended "Dos" and "Don'ts"

The following questions and recommended responses represent gratefully-received input from Human Resources managers, Diversity directors, members of gay, lesbian, bisexual, transgender, and queer Employee Resource Groups, and others in the field of diversity training and sexuality education from across the globe. The

"Dos" and "Don'ts" are simply suggestions for managers on how best to respond to lesbian, gay, bisexual, transgender, and queer issues as they arise in the workplace. If the recommended response doesn't seem to fit your particular situation, trust your instincts. Seek further input from your Human Resources office. You can also write me at brian@brian-mcnaught.com.

"So, what if…"

I don't know how to communicate the organization's policy?

Do **NOT** avoid talking about it and hope that everyone understands it anyway.

Do **NOT** send a memo simply telling people what the policy is without a *complete* explanation.

DO call a staff meeting and follow it up with a memo.

DO say…"The organization wants you to know, and I want you to know, that we *value* the diversity represented in our workforce. Notice I said *value* and not tolerate or accommodate. It's our diversity that will give us the cutting edge in competition. I want each and every one of you to feel that who you are is respected not *despite* your gender, race, age, ethnicity, culture, religious beliefs, sexual orientation, gender identity, gender expression, or disability, but rather *because* of those factors. We have zero tolerance of any behavior on the part of anyone, including me, that makes any of you feel uncomfortable at work because of your status in any of the categories I just mentioned. I'm not asking anyone to change their personal beliefs, but I am insisting that we work as a team, treating every member with courtesy and professional respect. If you have any questions about what constitutes lack of courtesy or professional respect, I want you to come see me, or contact our Human Resources office. I want to assure you that I didn't call you together because I have received a complaint. I called you together because I want this to be the highest-producing, most cohesive group in the organization. Are there any questions? Thank you. I'll be following this up with a memo."

I disagree with organization's policy on this?

Do **NOT** communicate your feelings verbally or non-verbally to anyone other than to your Human Resources professional. You are entitled to your opinion but you were hired to be a team player. As a manager, you are expected to be an enthusiastic *leader* and a faithful conveyor of organizational policy.

DO let your Human Resources professional or Diversity specialist know of your feelings and ask for guidance on how to navigate the distance between your personal beliefs and your behavior at work.

DO ask for feedback from your Human Resources professional and Diversity specialist on how well your behaviors model the policy's message.

DO arrange for and/or attend diversity training on lesbian, gay, bisexual, transgender, and queer workplace issues.

I don't know the proper language?

Do **NOT** let your fear of making a mistake prompt you to avoid using the words *"gay," "lesbian," "bisexual," "transgender"* or *"queer."* Not using the proper language creates the impression of discomfort or disapproval.

Do **NOT** use the words *"alternative lifestyle,"* or *"sexual preference."* They suggest that a choice has been made and that the discrimination experienced by homosexuals, bisexuals, and transgender people is not as serious as that faced by people because of their race, where no choice has been made.

Do **NOT** overuse the acronym LGBTQ or GLBTQ. Begin your conversations by using the words "gay," "lesbian," "bisexual," "transgender," and "queer." Over-using the acronym can prevent others from becoming comfortable with the words. It can also minimize the uniqueness of the five distinct groups and lessen their equality to other groups for which you would never use an acronym. (e.g. BLA for blacks, Latinos, and Asians.)

Do **NOT** refer to a gay, lesbian, or queer person's partner as their *"roommate"* or *"friend."* Say, instead, *"spouse," "partner,"* or *'life partner."*

Do **NOT** use the word *"transvestite"* for someone who cross-dresses. Say, instead, *"cross dresser,"* or *"transgender person."*

DO ask for guidance from openly lesbian, gay, bisexual, transgender, and queer-identified people in your work group, in your organization's LGBTQ Employee Resource Group (ERG) or from your Human Resources professional or Diversity specialist.

DO use the word *"gay"* as an adjective. "He's a gay man," or "She's gay." But don't use it to refer to people who are transgender.

DO use the word *"lesbian"* as a noun or an adjective. "She's a lesbian," or "She's a lesbian woman."

DO use the word *"bisexual"* as a noun or as an adjective. "He's bisexual," or "She's a bisexual woman."

DO use the words *"spouse," "life partner," "partner," "significant other," "boyfriend,"* or *"girlfriend"* to refer to the love interest of your gay, lesbian, bisexual, and queer employees.

DO use the word *"transgender"* as an umbrella term to refer to all people whose gender identity or expression is different than the sex assigned to them at birth, and/or the cultural expectations of biological sex.

DO use the word *"transgender"* as an adjective. "He's a man who is transgender," or "She's a woman who is transgender."

DO use the term *"transsexual"* to refer to a person whose gender identity is different than the sex assigned at birth. A person who is transsexual does not identify as both genders. They identify as the sex other than the sex they were assigned at birth. Some transsexuals choose to *realign* or *transition* by living as the gender they have always believed themselves to be. As part of the transition, some people who are transsexual choose to have applicable medical services, and some do not.

DO use the term *"cross dresser"* to refer to people who do not see themselves as the other sex (or sometimes as either sex,) but rather on a gender continuum. They occasionally need to present themselves as the other gender.

DO be flexible, patient, good humored, caring, and professional as you are confronted with changing concepts of sex and gender, and changing vocabulary for self-identification. But don't make the mistake of assuming that using a term such as "queer" to identify one team member or customer means that every other LGBT person has embraced the Q.

I don't know what constitutes discrimination or harassment?

Do **NOT** let anything pass because you are unsure if it constitutes discrimination or harassment. If you think it might, it probably does.

Do **NOT** assume that there are no people present who would be offended by the harassing comments or behaviors.

Do **NOT** stay silent if the behavior takes place among employees, including independent contractors, outside the office, such as at a social outing, or on a road trip.

Do **NOT** discount harassment based upon sexual orientation and gender identity/expression. Instead, treat it exactly as you would sexual harassment or racial hostility.

Do **NOT** discount harassment based upon sexual orientation and gender identity/expression because of concerns about protecting religious beliefs. People are free to believe whatever they wish, such as feeling that divorce is wrong, but they are required to refrain from any behavior, including expressing their beliefs that would be experienced by others as unwelcoming. Excluding others also constitutes "unwelcoming behavior."

Do **NOT** wait for a complaint before you address unwelcoming working conditions.

DO ask for guidance from Human Resources but keep in mind that discrimination, harassment, or bullying covers a wide range of conduct, blatant and covert, such as the use of words, sounds, facial expressions and other body language to express disrespect or disapproval of homosexuality or of gay, lesbian, bisexual, or queer people. The same would be true of similarly inappropriate behaviors in response to transgender people. Put yourself in the shoes of each employee. Attempt to see the workplace from their vantage points. Don't interpret their laughter at a comment as approval or comfort.

DO assume that if there are no openly lesbian, gay, bisexual, transgender or queer people working in your office, or people who talk openly about their LGBTQ friends and family members, that the environment is probably unwelcoming.

I don't know how to behave proactively?

Do **NOT** lose your sense of patience with, and humor about yourself. Everyone is on a learning curve. Everyone will make mistakes. The important thing is to do something.

Do **NOT** forget how Elliot got E.T. out of the shed in the film *E.T.* What are your "Reese's Pieces?" What incentives do you take to get people to trust you?

DO speak positively about all issues of diversity at all occasions.

DO let your office space reflect your awareness of, and commitment to, valuing diversity by displaying books, posters, photographs, and buttons that underscore the theme.

DO go out of your way to talk with and sit with people you feel might be experiencing marginalization. You needn't speak about anything other than your favorite film. It is the "music" of your comfort level that will assure them and all others of your commitment to corporate values.

DO sponsor diversity trainings for your staff and encourage their participation in multi-cultural events being sponsored by others in the organization.

DO communicate that you value the involvement of staff in employee resource or business groups (ERGs), such as those for women, people with disabilities, and for those who are gay, lesbian, bisexual, transgender, or queer.

DO be aware of events of interest to your diverse staff and make mention of your awareness. Just as you might wish "Happy Hanukkah" to a Jewish staff member, and "Happy Kwanzaa," to a black staff member, be aware of the days of significance to gay, lesbian, bisexual, transgender, and queer employees, such as Gay Pride Day, and Transgender Day of Remembrance (about those who have lost their lives in hate crimes.)

DO see becoming culturally competent as essential to your success as a manager and as an organization.. All of the "Reese's Pieces" that are helpful in building office harmony will work equally well with the culturally diverse customer base.

I have employees with conservative religious views?

Do **NOT** assume that because an employee has conservative religious views they are uncomfortable working with gay, lesbian, bisexual, transgender, and queer colleagues, or unable to fully embrace the organization's goal of valuing diversity.

Do **NOT** assume that all of the employees with conservative religious views are heterosexual or cis-gender. Some lesbian, gay, bisexual, transgender, and queer people identify themselves as fundamentalist Christians, Orthodox Jews, and strict Muslims. There are LGBTQ Catholics, Baptists, and Mormons.

Do **NOT** forget that the company affirms that your employees have a right to ALL of their beliefs, regardless of the source of those beliefs. But, they have **NO** right to *impose* those beliefs on their colleagues or customers in *any* manner. They have a right to affirm themselves but not at the expense of someone else. They may identify themselves as Muslim, Christian, Jew, Hindu, Taoist, agnostic or atheist, but in so doing they can't make statements, or behave in any way, that would be unwelcoming to anyone else, present or not present.

DO affirm the employees' rights to personal beliefs and explain clearly the parameters within which they can, as an employee of the organization, express those beliefs.

DO remember that your gay, lesbian, bisexual, transgender and queer employees, and their family members and friends, are likely to have as strongly-held religious views as the employee whose beliefs make it challenging to embrace the organization's intent to value *all* diversity.

DO ask your Human Resources professional or Diversity specialist for a list of behaviors, such as distributing religious materials, or posting judgmental statements in their cubicles, that are prohibited. Make that information available to every member of your team so that there are no questions about what constitutes discrimination, bullying, or harassment on not just the issues of sexual orientation, and gender identity and expression, but on all matters of personal moral values, such as those about divorce, inter-racial or inter-faith marriage, the proper role of women, or of being a Christian, Muslim, Jew, Hindu, or in another system of belief.

DO refer an employee to a Human Resources professional or Diversity specialist if they are not satisfied with your explanation.

someone quotes the Bible or the Koran to me?

Do **NOT** quote it back to them or engage in a discussion of your religious beliefs. Quoting the Bible, the Koran, or any religious text to support a position that is offensive to others is generally considered harassment.

DO quote to them the organization's policy on valuing the diversity of every employee, the guidelines on what behaviors are considered discriminatory, and of how the organization expects every employee to support its values.

DO refer the employee to a Human Resources professional or Diversity specialist if they are not satisfied with your answer.

I'm dealing with cultural conflicts?

Do **NOT** lose sight of the goal of valuing all diversity nor of the organization's position that personal biases, regardless of the source, will not be allowed to impact the cohesiveness of the workforce.

Do **NOT** dismiss the employee's cultural concerns. They must feel as if they have been heard. They must feel as if their cultural perspective is *valued*. But they must also know the parameters for expressing those cultural perspectives. Their insights as they pertain to achieving the goals of the organization are welcome. Their biases are not. For instance, it would be helpful to hear "In my culture, it is challenging reaching lesbian, gay, bisexual, transgender, or queer consumers because LGBTQ people feel the need to remain in the closet." It is counterproductive to hear, "In my culture, homosexuality (or transgenderism) is considered unnatural and sinful."

DO ask for help from the employees in better understanding their cultural perspectives and how they would suggest maximizing the organization's goals of recruiting talent in their culture and of effectively marketing to their culture.

DO provide training for all of your team on the cultural diversity represented in your work group. Ask your Human Resources professional or Diversity specialist on how best to do so.

DO help your team understand and affirm the personal challenges faced in creating cohesion in a diverse workforce.

the law in my country prohibits homosexual behavior?

Do **NOT** confuse sexual *behavior* with the *status* of sexual orientation or sexual identity. If a country prohibits homosexual behavior, the organization's non-discrimination policies and benefits packages do NOT violate local laws, as the organization takes NO position on personal, private behavior. For instance, the law of a country might also prohibit inter-racial marriage or divorce. That does not mean that the organization cannot hire and treat with professional respect people who have the status of being inter-racially married or divorced. The organization's policy does not encourage or discourage divorce, procreation, religious beliefs, sexual behaviors, inter-faith, or inter-racial marriage. It seeks to attract and retain talented people who may or may not fit into categories because of their private behaviors. If the organization is not state or church-owned, it has no responsibility to reflect the beliefs of the state or the church regarding people's private behaviors. Nor does the state or the church have rightful jurisdiction over the private organization's policies.

DO explain these distinctions to your work group. If you have further questions, contact your Human Resources professional, and/or a representative from your Legal department.

my boss is hostile to the issue?

Do **NOT** try to change the mind or values of your boss with personal arguments, but do **NOT** let pass anything inappropriate they say or do about gay, lesbian, bisexual, transgender, or queer people (or any other groups.) You're in a tough position. You have the complete support of your executive leadership and your Human Resources professionals, but you report to a person who has enormous impact on the happiness of your daily life and on your career. Nevertheless, if you are also a manager, you set yourself up for organizational discipline if you're seen as complicit in creating a hostile work environment.

DO contact your Human Resources professional or Diversity specialist and ask for guidance. (You may be able to register your concern anonymously.) If you are a manager, they may suggest that you meet privately with your boss and say, "I have the feeling that this is an issue with which you do not feel total comfort. As you know, the people at the top take compliance on this very seriously. It's not an issue that causes me any problems. I have family and friends who are gay (or transgender.) I'd be happy to be the point person if something comes up, to take the lead in talking to the group about the issue, and to be a resource to you if you should need one." If such a discussion is not possible, the Human Resources professional will suggest other steps that can be taken that protect your anonymity.

DO suggest to the boss and to the department as a whole that diversity training on all issues, including sexual orientation and gender identity/expression would be of use to them in better understanding what is expected of them in separating their personal beliefs from their behaviors.

our best client is homophobic or transphobic?

Do **NOT** abandon organizational principles for financial gain. In the short run, it may feel as if you made the right decision. In the long run, being unclear of what is acceptable behavior will come back to haunt you. Deal with it before it becomes too big a deal.

Do **NOT** try to change the mind or the values of your client. They are entitled to their beliefs. If they engage in behaviors that would be unwelcome to anyone in your organization, in a non-confrontative manner, communicate yours and the organization's feelings about the issue. That can be as subtle as not laughing at a joke or comment, changing the subject, explaining the organization's position on valuing *all* diversity, and/or sharing how the comments make you feel personally.

DO seek support from your Human Resources professional and from your manager. If the homophobia or transphobia is being expressed by the client's CEO it may require an inquiring personal call from your CEO who asks, "As is undoubtedly true with you, our workforce is multi-cultural, which is how we like it. I just want to make sure that you're open to working with our best and brightest, regardless of their race, gender, religion, sexual orientation, or gender identity or expression." If the homophobia or transphobia is being expressed by an employee of the client, it may simply require requesting that you be given a different contact with whom you can work.

Our best client won't work with our lesbian, gay, bisexual, transgender or queer employee?

Do **NOT** do anything until you have spoken to a Human Resources professional or Diversity specialist.

Do **NOT** support the client by saying you understand why it would be hard for them to work with your gay, lesbian, bisexual, transgender or queer employee, and do **NOT** try to talk them into working with your LGBTQ employee. Affirm your organization's goal of valuing all diversity, and acknowledge that you want it to be a good working relationship, and that such a relationship requires comfort.

Do **NOT** assign someone to replace the lesbian, gay, bisexual, transgender, or queer-identified employee, but if you must, first talk to the employee in question and explain to them the situation with the client, your complete faith in the competence of the employee, and your disappointment in the client's shortsightedness. Ask for the employee's support in the decision you feel is necessary, and ask for their guidance in who would be the next best person, with regard to expertise, to work directly with the client.

DO affirm the talents of the lesbian, gay, bisexual, transgender, or queer employee with the client, citing other clients who work happily with them. Communicate the organization's policy of valuing all diversity. Tell them who their contact will now be and why you feel they will work well with them. Remind them that the LGBTQ employee remains available to help out if necessary.

someone in my group comes out to me as lesbian, gay bisexual, transgender, or queer?

Do **NOT** look away, take any calls, allow any interruptions, or close the blinds.

Do **NOT** say, "It makes no difference to me," (it does to them or they wouldn't have told you), "I never would have known," (what does a LGBTQ person look like?), "I love the sinner but hate the sin," (your religious views are irrelevant), "What a waste," (from whose perspective?), "Why do I need to know? I don't talk about what I do in bed? Why must you talk about what you do in bed?" (It's not about "sex." It's about personhood.)

DO look them in the eye, smile, breathe, and thank them for telling you.

DO say, "I'm glad that you felt you could tell me. Have you shared the information with anyone else? It's between us unless you tell me otherwise. How can I support you? Have there been any problems in the office I haven't been aware of? Are you aware of our organization's commitment to value the diversity you bring to the table as a gay (or transgender) person? Have you connected with our lesbian, gay, bisexual, transgender, and queer Employee Resource Group? Would you like to?"

DO discuss providing diversity training for the department.

someone I think is lesbian, gay, bisexual, transgender, or queer won't come out?

Do **NOT** assume that everyone who is gay, lesbian, bisexual, transgender, or queer wants to come out. The issue for you is "Could they safely do so if they wanted to do so?"

Do **NOT** ask the person if they are lesbian, gay, bisexual, transgender, or queer in front of others, or in anything other than a supportive, non-intrusive way, and never ask solely to satisfy your curiosity. Instead, ask because you want to help them feel safe and valued.

Do **NOT** change your behavior around them, unless your behavior has been hostile.

Do **NOT** assume that they are the only lesbian, gay, bisexual, transgender or queer person in the office.

DO continue to create an environment that you think would make a lesbian, gay, bisexual, transgender, or queer person feel safe and valued. Use inclusive language at staff meetings and in social conversations, such as using the term "family" in its broadest possible sense, and inquiring if a person has a partner rather than "Are you married?"

DO ask for guidance from your Human Resources professional or Diversity specialist and educate your team by providing good diversity training on LGBTQ issues, among other topics.

DO think about your "music." How easy do you think it might be for someone to tell you that they're lesbian, gay, bisexual, transgender, or queer? What are your "Reese's Pieces?"

what if someone in the group appears to be transgender?

Do **NOT** ask about the person's gender identity or expression. If you have an employee who is in the process, or who wants to *realign* or *transition*, they will likely come to you and alert you to what is transpiring in their lives *if* they feel they can trust you. If they plan to have medical assistance, standard practice recommended by medical and sexuality professionals is to live openly for a year as the gender with which they emotionally identify. Thus, in order to qualify for the operation, they **must** dress in their new gender on a daily basis, use a gender-appropriate name (and thus need to change their security pass, if such passes exist in your organization,) need to use the restroom that is appropriate to their gender identity, and need to have the understanding and support of their colleagues. If the employee is not transsexual but seeks to express both genders with which they identify on an irregular basis, assume that they too will likely approach you to discuss their need to cross-dress before doing so if your "music" suggests that you will support them.

Do **NOT** ignore the issue if you sense that an employee is moving forward with realignment or transition without alerting you, or if you sense that there is disruption in the cohesion of the workforce. Before taking any action, ask your Human Resources professional or diversity specialist for guidance. Determine first if the organization has policies or practices that prohibit discrimination based upon gender identity (sex realignment/transsexual) and gender expression (presentation of gender.)

DO explore your own feelings about a person being transsexual, and the diversity of gender expression. Consider what "music" you have on these issues so that you'll know how effective you might be in addressing the issue one-on-one with the employee. If you feel completely comfortable and trust your instincts, bring the employee in for a discussion. If you do not feel comfortable or confident, ask for help from Human Resources in addressing the issue.

DO make the meeting with the employee you believe is transgender feel completely safe for the employee. If necessary, offer to meet off site. Consider starting the discussion by saying, "The reason that I've asked you to get together is to see how I might best support you as your mentor at work. I've noticed, and perhaps I'm wrong, that you are varying your personal presentation at work, (which is completely your right, as you know. Our organization prohibits discrimination based upon gender expression) such as…" wearing more androgynous clothing, androgynous hair style, earrings, perfume, make-up, etc. "Am I right or am I way off base?" If the answer is "You're off base," consider saying, "Okay, I apologize if I've offended you in any way. My intention was merely to show support, but I want you to know that there has been some office speculation. I thought perhaps I'd sponsor a diversity program on a variety of issues, including gender expression, so that all of us are clear that how a person expresses their gender at work is not a criterion for measuring their contribution to the team. What do you think about that?" If, on the other hand, they say "Thank you for bringing this up. I have been wanting to talk with you about it," consider saying "Thank you for affirming that for me. Now, how can I help you? How can we together make the office feel as safe and productive as possible for you and for everyone else? I've been thinking we need a diversity presentation on gender identity and expression. Would that make you feel uncomfortable or do you agree that it will help us all move forward?"

DO remember that if the person who is transgender does come out to you, the information *must* be kept completely confidential. The transgender person is typically very concerned about how the information will be disclosed to the rest of the organization when they are ready to be out, and if the rest of the team will treat them differently.

my organization doesn't have a policy on gender identity or expression?

Do **NOT** assume that there are no local laws governing the issue, or soon won't be.

Do **NOT** assume that your organization never will have such a policy. Inquire of your Human Resources professional why the organization doesn't have such a policy or practice. Lobby for such inclusion.

Do **NOT** assume that there are no transgender or queer people in your office or among your clients.

DO speak and behave as if your organization had such a policy or practice, and as if you had a transgender or queer person in your office and among your clients.

DO ask your Diversity or Human Resources professional for guidance and training on this issue. Stay ahead of the game.

a lesbian, gay, bisexual, transgender, or queer employee wants to be out and I don't think that it's safe?

Do **NOT** assume that what would feel unsafe for you would necessarily feel unsafe for your colleague. Tell them of your concern and your reasons for judging the environment to be unsafe. Ask for their assessment of the environment.

Do **NOT** make it more difficult for them to come out by suggesting that if they do so, "You're on your own." Instead, tell them that whatever they decide to do, you will back them up.

Do **NOT** assume that they want you to tell other people for them. Ask them if there is anything you can do to make it easier, including telling others for them.

Do **NOT** say, "I told you so," if things work out poorly for the colleague who is coming out. They are being harassed because of their status, not as a result of anything they are doing wrong. It is not their fault if others respond unprofessionally, and in violation of organizational policies and ideals.

DO proactively address the conditions that prompt you to feel that it is not safe for this employee, or any employee, to be out at work.

DO ask for guidance from your Human Resources professional and Diversity specialist. Tell them of your concerns. See if they share your views. Come up with a strategy that supports the decision of the gay, lesbian, bisexual, transgender, or queer colleague and promote an inclusive climate for all employees.

DO your best to create a safer environment by communicating clearly the organization's expectations of every employee to *value* diversity. Be clear of what that means in day-to-day behaviors. Tell them that such support of their LGBTQ colleague is expected inside and outside of the office, when on organizational business, and always with clients.

DO put the lesbian, gay, bisexual, transgender, or queer colleague in touch with the LGBTQ Employee Resource Group (ERG) for support. Encourage them to contact the Human Resources or your Diversity specialist for information on sources of support outside of the organization.

DO provide diversity training on gay, lesbian, bisexual, transgender, and queer issues for your staff.

an LGBTQ employee tells a gay or transgender joke, or uses prohibited language?

Do **NOT** encourage the behavior by laughing at the joke, or indicating that the language is acceptable. Treat the situation exactly as you would if the joke or offensive language was coming from the mouth of a heterosexual or a cis-gender person.

Do **NOT** accept that the lesbian, gay, bisexual, transgender, or queer person telling the joke or using objectionable language, such as "fag," "dyke," "queer," "homo," "queen," or "tranny" has license to make fun of themselves. Their language undermines office cohesion, confuses heterosexual colleagues, and offends other LGBTQ people, and those who love and support them. Their behavior does not represent the feelings of the organization's LGBTQ Employee Resource Group, even if it is coming from a member or officer of the ERG. Some lesbian, gay, bisexual, transgender, and queer people can be immature and unsophisticated. Some suffer from internalized homophobia or transphobia. Being LGBTQ does not give them permission to defy the organization's efforts to *value* diversity.

DO speak up in such situations to express your discomfort and disappointment. Take the lead in showing others that this behavior or language is not acceptable.

DO pull the gay, lesbian, bisexual, transgender, or queer person aside and tell them what about their behavior is unacceptable and why: "It gives license to others to behave the same way, and it creates a hostile working environment for others."

DO report the incident to your Human Resources or Diversity specialist. Make sure that you have their support so that you don't hear from them later that the lesbian, gay, bisexual, transgender, or queer person felt discriminated against or "put down."

I don't have any lesbian, gay, bisexual, transgender, or queer people in my group or client base?

Do **NOT** make such assumptions. Even if you're correct, which is unlikely, *always* assume that you do have gay, lesbian, bisexual, transgender, and queer people present so that your language and behavior creates a welcoming environment.

Do **NOT** assume that no one in the office has a personal connection to someone who is lesbian, gay, bisexual, transgender, or queer, or that they would tell you about it if they didn't think you were fully supportive.

Do **NOT** assume that none of your clients are lesbian, gay, bisexual, transgender, or queer, or have personal connections to people who are LGBTQ.

Do **NOT** expect that a fully integrated transsexual will feel it necessary or useful to discuss his or her status as a transsexual. If they are seen by others as the gender with which they identify, they are generally ready to move on with their lives. They are likely to see themselves, and to be seen by others, as male or female, as the case may be.

Do **NOT** assume that you can identify gay people. Most gay, lesbian, bisexual, and queer people do not satisfy cultural stereotypes, and sometimes heterosexual people satisfy those gay stereotypes.

Do **NOT** assume that everyone who is gay, lesbian, bisexual, transgender or queer *wants* to come out. Some LGBTQ people, like some heterosexual and cis-gender people, are very private about their personal lives not out of fear, but rather out of personal preference.

DO proceed as if you do have someone in your office or your client base who is lesbian, gay, bisexual, transgender, or queer, or who has a personal connection to an LGBTQ person, and remind your colleagues what behaviors are considered welcoming and what are considered unwelcoming.

the lesbian, gay, bisexual, transgender, or queer person's job performance is the problem?

Do **NOT** be intimidated by the person's minority status. If their job performance is unsatisfactory, respond as you would with anyone else. If you don't, you'll create resentment among the rest of the staff who will feel victimized by you and the gay, lesbian, bisexual, transgender, or queer person. That is not good for morale or productivity. The goal in all of the organization's diversity initiatives is equal treatment, not special treatment.

Do **NOT** forget that you are the person's mentor. As you would with anyone else, set aside the issues of sexual orientation, gender, race, age, religion, disability, or any other factor, treat them as adults who are expected to act responsibly, and work with them to solve the problem.

DO speak first to your Diversity and Human Resources professional to let them know what's going on, and ask for their input on how to handle the situation.

DO speak to the individual in private, clearly state what you see as the problem, ask them for their perspective, tell them what you expect of them, and set up a time to meet again to evaluate their progress.

DO ask if they find the office environment to be welcoming, and if they trust that you value the diversity they bring to the table.

the transgender or queer person wants to use the "wrong" restroom?

Do **NOT** do a thing until you've checked with your Diversity or Human Resources specialist to ascertain the organization's policy. If the organization doesn't have a restroom policy, insist that the Human Resources specialist contact an organization known for its "best practice." The "best practice" is to have the transgender or queer person use the restroom that matches their current gender expression.

Do **NOT** assume that you, the transgender or queer person, and the organization agree on the appropriateness of the word "wrong."

Do **NOT** assume that this issue is a small, insignificant matter. The use of the sex-appropriate restroom has enormous emotional and political meaning to the transgender or queer person, most particularly those who are in the process of realignment.

Do **NOT** assume that this issue has no significance to others. Some women feel unsafe if there is a biological male in their restroom. This is more likely to be a concern if we're talking about a transgender person who cross-dresses at work on occasion. It's a different matter, for some, if the person is transsexual.

Do **NOT** ask a person if they have had surgery. That is a personal matter. The transgender or queer person may or may not choose to share that information. But it is not helpful to make decisions about appropriate restroom use based upon those criteria, as many transsexuals and queer people opt not to have surgery for a variety of reasons, the high cost of the medical services being one of them.

Do **NOT** ask a transgender or queer person to use a restroom that is not conveniently located.

DO find a solution to the restroom issue that is safe, dignified, and convenient.

DO communicate to the transgender or queer person and to your cisgender colleagues that you understand this issue can be emotionally charged.

DO communicate with the employee who is uncomfortable in the same restroom as a transgender or queer person that they are being heard. Consider saying, "I understand your feelings, and I want to make sure that you are comfortable using our restrooms. Like most of our competitors, our policy is that the transgender or queer person will use the restroom that is appropriate to the gender they're presenting. I hope that we can work together as a team on this so that everyone in our group feels valued. Can I ask you, as a first step, to either use another restroom that is conveniently located or to try to use the restroom when your colleague who is transgender is not using it? If you continue to feel uncomfortable, and it interferes with your work, please come see me. I think it might be good if we had some diversity training on this issue. I know that I would find it helpful."

DO ask for help from your Diversity or Human Resources professional to explain the organization's policy on restroom use to your staff.

DO provide diversity training on transgender and queer issues to your staff before this issue comes up.

DO periodically check in with the transgender or queer employee, and with one or two staff members, to see how the situation is going.

DO make sure that this issue doesn't negatively impact the productivity of the office or undermine the organization's commitment to value diversity.

we need training and someone refuses to participate?

Do **NOT** underestimate the enormous emotional, psychological, spiritual, and political significance of this issue for everyone in the office. Handle with care.

Do **NOT** communicate a lack of awareness or sensitivity to the feelings of everyone on your staff, but do not coddle behaviors that undermine the values of the organization.

Do **NOT** accommodate a threat to office cohesion in the name of personal moral values. If you allow an employee to absent themselves from diversity training on LGBTQ issues without ramifications, you communicate that the organization's values are negotiable, and you set a precedent for the behavior of the staff on all other organizational initiatives.

Do **NOT** be afraid to confront bias on gay, lesbian, bisexual, transgender, or queer issues that are couched in religious views anymore than you would avoid confronting racism or sexism that are couched in statements about "freedom of religion." The organization respects the diversity of religious views but does not embrace any one religion's doctrines. The organization seeks to create an environment in which people of varying religious views can work comfortably together as a team. Consider providing training on the diversity of religious views.

DO ask for help from your Diversity and Human Resources professional. Ask them for the organization's policy on mandatory attendance.

DO be consistent. If you have not mandated training on sexual harassment, do **not** mandate attendance at diversity training on LGBT issues. If you *have* mandated training on sexual harassment or other issues of diversity, do **not** make training on lesbian, gay, bisexual, transgender, and queer issues optional.

DO communicate your unequivocal commitment to valuing diversity, and to creating a workplace in which all employees feel safe and valued.

DO talk one-on-one with the employee who refuses to attend the training to see if you can eliminate any preconceived notions they have of the training. Provide them literature about the trainer and the program. Provide them feedback to the training from others who have heard the presentation. Ask them to come and sit with you for the first hour. Assure them that their religious values will not be assaulted.

DO explain that the entire office is attending the training as a team and that if they chose to absent themselves from the activity it reflects their lack of interest in the team. Such behavior makes them less attractive for positions of leadership.

DO explain that the training will outline which behaviors at work are considered supportive and welcoming of lesbian, gay, bisexual, transgender and queer colleagues and which behaviors are considered unwelcoming and forbidden by organization policy. Make clear that if the employee chooses to absent themself from the training and then inadvertently engages in behaviors that are considered hostile, that they cannot use ignorance or lack of awareness of the policy as an excuse, and that action will be taken.

legal action is threatened?

Do **NOT** say anything more about the issue to the person threatening legal action. Immediately refer the matter to the Legal department and to the Human Resources office. Inform the person in question that you are unable, for legal reasons, to discuss the issue further.

Do **NOT** change your behavior toward the person threatening legal action. Keep the issue separate. Focus on the organization's ideals of teamwork that values diversity.

DO make clear to your colleagues your intention to maintain office cohesiveness. Discourage any discussion of the issue, explaining that it has been referred to the company's legal counsel.

I'm gay, lesbian, bisexual, or queer?

Do **NOT** hide the fact that you're gay, lesbian, bisexual, or queer unless you feel you have no options. Incorporate your personal life into your life in the office in the same way you would if you were heterosexual. If you are known by some to be LGBTQ, but are not out at work, you send a clear message that the environment is unwelcoming.

Do **NOT** feel that being gay, lesbian, bisexual, or queer requires you to be the "answer person" on LGBT issues in the workplace. You were hired because of your skills, not because you're lesbian, gay, bisexual, or queer. Explain that being lesbian, gay, bisexual, or queer doesn't make you an authority on LGBTQ workplace issues and request diversity training for your team from your Human Resources professional or Diversity specialist.

Do **NOT** accommodate inappropriate behavior in the office because you want to be accepted by the team.

DO see your sexual orientation as a gift to the company. Explore what unique contributions you have to make because of your experiences as a gay man, lesbian woman, bisexual or queer person. If the organization is serious about *valuing* diversity, it feels that your diversity represents a unique value. What is it?

DO consider joining the LGBTQ Employee Resource Group (ERG).

DO be aware that the messenger *is* the message. Like it or not, people who don't know other gay, lesbian, bisexual or queer people are watching you to decide how comfortable they feel with homosexuals and bisexuals.

I'm transgender, or queer?

Do **NOT** accommodate inappropriate behaviors because you want to be accepted. You were hired for your skills and performance, not your gender identity or expression.

Do **NOT** feel that you have to be the "transgender or queer answer person." Arrange for your colleagues to participate in diversity training on transgender and queer issues.

DO see your transgender or queer status as a gift to the organization. Beyond your ability to help the organization market their product to the transgender and queer community, your diversity represents a unique life perspective that the organization says it values. Think about what strengths you bring to the table.

DO consider joining the LGBTQ Employee Resource Group (ERG).

DO be aware that the messenger *is* the message. Most people do not know someone who is transgender or queer. Like it or not, you represent all transsexuals, cross-dressers, or queer people to your colleagues.

the organization isn't a safe place for lesbian, gay, bisexual, transgender or queer employees?

Do **NOT** let it *stay* unsafe for your sake, for that of your gay, lesbian, bisexual, transgender, or queer employees, and for that of the organization's productivity and reputation. Do something about it.

Do **NOT** assume that you are the only one who has noticed its unwelcoming atmosphere. You have allies.

DO speak to your Diversity or Human Resources professional about your concerns and ask for diversity training in your department.

DO speak up as often as you can in as many work-related situations as possible to communicate your interest in creating a safe and productive work environment. It sometimes takes just one strong-willed heterosexual or cis-gender ally to turn an organization around.

DO share your feelings privately with gay, lesbian, bisexual, transgender, and queer employees, and offer to be a source of support to them in both public and private ways.

DO avoid using the term "hostile" to describe the workplace, as it carries legal implications, unless of course you feel the environment *is* "hostile" and you are willing to say so in legal proceedings.

the office of Human Resources is of no help to me?

Do **NOT** assume that because a person works in Human Resources (HR) or in Diversity that they are knowledgeable or skilled on all issues of diversity. Do **NOT** assume that every person in HR or in Diversity is even sensitive or sympathetic to every issue. As in every department, HR and Diversity employees reflect their education, religious beliefs, culture, family dynamics, and their exposure to people different from themselves.

Do **NOT** assume that an initial lack of support or interest means that you don't have a potential ally. Most people in HR have their heart in the right place. They want to create a workplace that feels safe and productive for everyone.

DO tell the director of HR of your needs and of your experience of a lack of support on the issue. Ask them for their opinion on the attitudes in the department, and suggest diversity training on lesbian, gay, bisexual, transgender, and queer issues for the entire staff. Recommend that they contact the Human Rights Campaign (www.hrc.org) in the United States, Stonewall (www.stonewall.org.uk) in the United Kingdom, Egale (www.egale.ca) in Canada, or other human resource professionals in other parts of your organization, or in other organizations. They can also contact me at brian@brian-mcnaught.com.

DO take action if you do not get a satisfactory response from your Office of Human Resources. Speak to your manager and to the organization's global director of HR. If necessary, contact a member of the Executive Steering Committee. The lack of sophistication and support on these issues in the Human Resources department will have a negative impact on the organization's ability to attract and retain the best and brightest employees, its productivity, and its marketability to all consumers.

I manage lesbian, gay, bisexual, transgender, or queer people in a country with hostile cultural attitudes on the issues?

Do **NOT** focus on changing the local culture. Focus instead on making sure that within the office, the atmosphere feels safe to the lesbian, gay, bisexual, transgender and queer employees, and that they trust you understand the challenges they face outside of the office walls.

Do **NOT** allow the hostility of the local culture to intimidate you. While you may be a guest in their country or a native, you are also a representative of your organization in that country. Your job is to guarantee that the organization's values are clearly expressed and realized in all business dealings.

Do **NOT** tolerate hostile comments from clients regarding lesbian, gay, bisexual, transgender, or queer issues. All persons connected with your organization need to see you as a strong, clear voice of support.

DO understand that the hostility of the local culture toward gay, lesbian, bisexual, and queer people is to homosexual *behavior*, **not** homosexual *orientation* or *identity*. Your organization takes no position on homosexual behavior, anymore than it does on divorce, inter-racial marriage, the one "true" religion, worship practices, or the role of women in marriages. It does, though, protect from discrimination persons because of their status (orientation and/or identity) as gay, transgender, divorced, inter-racially married, Muslim, Christian, or female. There is no conflict between local legal or social practices and the organization's policy of valuing diversity.

DO provide diversity training and educational resources on LGBTQ issues to your staff. Disseminate all statements of support from the organization's headquarters.

DO help create a local chapter of the organization's lesbian, gay, bisexual, transgender, and queer Employee Resource Group (ERG) even if all of its local members identify as heterosexual and cis-gender. Sponsor events on the topic and network with the LGBTQ ERGs of other corporations in the area.

DO remember that your success in creating a safe and welcoming environment in which lesbian, gay, bisexual, transgender, and queer employees feel valued should not be measured by how many LGBTQ people come out. Given the hostility of the local culture, it is not likely that many LGBTQ people from that culture will feel comfortable identifying themselves. Coming out is more likely to happen with lesbian, gay, bisexual, transgender, and queer employees from supportive cultures who happen to be working in your office. Nevertheless, always assume that there is an LGBTQ person in your office, whether or not they self-identify.

DO consider sending your lesbian, gay, bisexual, transgender, and queer staff members, and your heterosexual and cis-gender Diversity and Human Resource professionals to the annual workplace conference of Out and Equal (www.outandequal.org) that is held in the United States. It provides education and the opportunity for networking to gay, lesbian, bisexual, transgender, queer, cis-gender, and heterosexual employees from around the world. Similar conferences are held in different countries. Ask your local LGBTQ ERG leadership for guidance in finding such resources.

I want to transfer a lesbian, gay, bisexual, transgender, or queer employee to an office in a country with hostile cultural attitudes on the issues?

Do **NOT** do so without consulting with the gay, lesbian, bisexual, transgender, or queer employee to determine if they want to consider taking the assignment.

Do **NOT** assume that because the culture is hostile that the LGBTQ employee would *not* want to go. However, be sure to find out what the laws in the area are regarding homosexuality and transgenderism.

Do **NOT** make assumptions about the culture. Many places around the world have reputations of being unwelcoming but the atmosphere has changed for the better. Check with the Human Resources professional and Diversity specialist in the region and with the LGBTQ Employee Resource Group (ERG) should there be one in the area.

Do **NOT** send the lesbian, gay, bisexual, transgender, or queer employee to the region without asking their permission to notify their future manager of the situation.

DO talk at length with the lesbian, gay, bisexual, transgender, or queer employee as to why you want to send them to the region, why you feel it would be good for the organization, and why it would be good for them, if you believe it to be.

DO ask what reservations the lesbian, gay, bisexual, transgender, or queer employee might have about working in the office in the new region, such as whether there is a support community, attitudes of his new manager and the local HR representative toward LGBTQ issues, the timeframe of the assignment, and what they would do if they entered a relationship prior to the assignment or while on assignment.

the lesbian, gay, bisexual, transgender, or queer person I want to transfer has a spouse/partner?

Do **NOT** assume that it will be easy for either person to relocate, even if it is to a place in the world known for its welcoming attitude toward LGBTQ people.

Do **NOT** assume that the gay, lesbian, bisexual, transgender, or queer couple is *not* interested.

DO check on immigration laws. Can the couple immigrate as a couple? Do both individuals need work permits? What work is now done by the spouse/partner of your LGBTQ employee and how will they continue to make a living in the new location?

DO plan, even if your country's laws don't require it, on paying all relocation expenses for both members of the relationship, just as you would if the employee was in a heterosexual partnership.

DO prepare the office to which they are being sent for the arrival of a lesbian, gay, bisexual, transgender, or queer couple, should the employee consent to such notification. Seek support in advance from the Human Resources professional, Diversity specialist, and LGBTQ Employee Resource Group in the new area.

DO prepare to help your lesbian, gay, bisexual, transgender, or queer employee if they enter a relationship with a foreign national while on assignment and wants to return to your home office to work.

I have a parent or spouse of a lesbian, gay, bisexual, transgender, or queer person, and they need help?

Do **NOT** take lightly their need for help. If they are troubled by the issue, it will impact their productivity and that of the team. Their difficulties are a business concern.

DO communicate with the employee that you take seriously their situation, that you support them completely in addressing their concern, and that you do so without judgment or personal bias.

DO contact the Human Resources office, the Diversity specialist, and the leadership of the organization's LGBTQ Employee Resource Group and ask for help. They can provide you with local resources and offer to meet with and support the employee who needs help. Local resources can include support groups, therapists, literature, social events, and mentoring options.

DO follow-up with the employee to ensure that they are getting the support that they need.

I want to recruit talented lesbian, gay, bisexual, transgender, and queer employees?

Do **NOT** think your competition isn't trying to do the same. They are showing up at college career days, setting up booths, and displaying literature that shows their support of LGBTQ issues. They are also attending meetings of, and making presentations at professional conferences that attract lesbian, gay, bisexual, transgender, and queer employees, such as those held annually by Out and Equal in the U.S., and more regularly by local LGBTQ business organizations. Some organizations are placing large display ads in national print media read by lesbian, gay, bisexual, transgender, and queer people, or on the Internet. Most organizations that seek LGBTQ talent are underscoring their commitment to valuing diversity on their organizational web sites.

DO consult with your LGBTQ Employee Resource Group (ERG), your Human Resources professional, and your Diversity specialist and ask for help in achieving your goals.

I want to be an ally?

Do **NOT** assume you aren't already an ally. By asking the question, you show that you are.

Do **NOT** pass up an opportunity to show to others at work that you are an ally by doing such things as refusing to laugh at anti-gay or anti-transgender humor, by speaking up if others are discussing the issues, by raising the issue yourself in staff meetings, by requesting diversity training on the issues in your department, by using inclusive language ("Do you have a partner?" instead of "Are you married?"), by sitting with lesbian, gay, bisexual, transgender and queer people in the cafeteria and figuring out a way to make the LGBTQ people feel more welcome at organization social events, and by not being afraid to be mistaken as lesbian, gay, bisexual, transgender, or queer by others because of your strong support.

DO contact the organization's existing LGBT Employee Resource Group and tell them that you'd like to be a member. If there is not a LGBTQ ERG in your location, contact the Human Resources office or your Diversity specialist and tell them of your interest in starting a local chapter.

I need outside help?

DO contact me at brian@brian-mcnaught.com.

Bottom Line:

Your organization values diversity because doing so is good for business. The increased productivity profits everyone. The organization seeks to attract and retain the best and brightest employees by creating a safe and productive work environment that affirms rather than accommodates differences. The organization expects all of its employees to manifest its commitment of respect for all.

One can personally disagree with the organization's policies and practices regarding sexual orientation and gender identity or expression, but it's not acceptable to express those feelings at work in any manner that undermines the organization's goals.

Feel your feelings but choose your behaviors. You are expected to treat all employees with professional respect and courtesy, and to actively create an environment that maximizes the productivity of the entire team.

About the Author:

Brian McNaught is a certified sexuality educator, diversity trainer, and author whose primary focus are the issues facing gay, lesbian, bisexual, transgender, and queer people, and those who live or work with them. Named "the godfather of gay sensitivity training" by the *New York Times* in 1993, he has worked primarily with heterosexual audiences in major corporations and university settings around the world since 1974. His clients include over 200 universities, nearly every major financial institution in New York, London, and the Pacific Rim, as well as a significant representation of other Fortune 50 businesses. Brian has also presented at the National Security Agency (NSA), government research facilities, and the Federal Reserve.

The middle child of seven Irish Catholics from Detroit, Michigan, Brian is the product of sixteen years of parochial education. He received his degree in journalism from Marquette University in 1970, was a staff writer, columnist, and talk show host for the Archdiocese of Detroit, and lost his job when he affirmed being gay in 1974. He later served as the Mayor of Boston's liaison to the gay and lesbian community, worked with the National Council of Churches and the National Conference of Catholic Bishops on young adult ministry, and served as an advisor to former U.S. Surgeon

General David Satcher on his national sexual health initiative entitled "A Call to Action."

Brian is the author of the classic "coming out" book, *On Being Gay – Thoughts on Family, Faith, and Love,* as well as *Gay Issues in the Workplace*, and *Now That I'm Out, What Do I Do?* His popular book *"Sex Camp,"* like his other works, is used as a college text. *Are You Guys Brothers?* focuses on the dynamics and issues in any relationship, through the lens of his partnership with Ray Struble since 1976.. Brian also produced and/or is featured in seven highly praised DVDs, three of which have aired regularly on Public Broadcasting Stations in the United States. His two-hour DVD presentation entitled *"Gay and Transgender Issues in the Workplace,"* is used extensively in global diversity efforts. He wrote the script and facilitator's guide, and hosts the DVD "Anyone Can Be an Ally – Speaking Up for an LGBTQ Inclusive Workplace." He and Ray, a retired Managing Director of global equity sales for Lehman Brothers, divide their year between Tupper Lake, NY, and Ft. Lauderdale, FL.

To contact Brian, or to learn more about his many cost-free books, DVDs, and other resources, go to www.brian-mcnaught.com.

Made in the USA
Las Vegas, NV
09 June 2023

73177683R00042